Playmakers

Basketball Centers

Tom Greve

ROURKE PUBLISHING

Vero Beach, Florida 32964

www.rourkepublishing.com

PHOTO CREDITS: © strickke: Title Page, 10, 11, 15, 17; © Brandon Laufenberg: Illustrations; © Associated Press: 5, 7, 9, 12, 13, 18, 19; © Bill Grove: 8; © Gary Milner: 2; © Nikada: 22

Editor: Jeanne Sturm

Cover and page design by Tara Raymo

Library of Congress Cataloging-in-Publication Data

Greve, Tom.
Basketball centers / Tom Greve.
p. cm. -- (Playmakers)
Includes index.
ISBN 978-1-60694-330-4 (hard cover)
ISBN 978-1-60694-829-3 (soft cover)
1. Center play (Basketball)--Juvenile literature. 2. Centers (Basketball)--United States--Biography--Juvenile literature. I. Title.
GV887.74.G74 2010
796.323068--dc22
2009006017

Printed in the USA

CG/CG

ROURKE PUBLISHING

www.rourkepublishing.com - rourke@rourkepublishing.com
Post Office Box 643328 Vero Beach, Florida 32964

Table of Contents

Whether it is called **patrolling** the paint, playing the **pivot,** or even manning the middle, basketball centers usually stand out. Centers are often the tallest players on the court. They score, **rebound,** and block shots for their team.

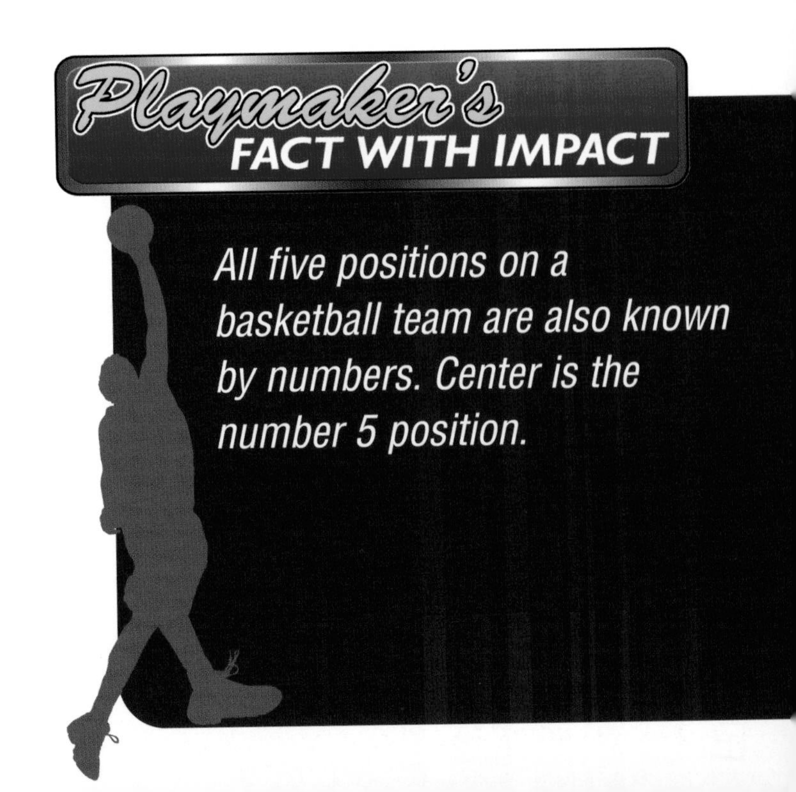

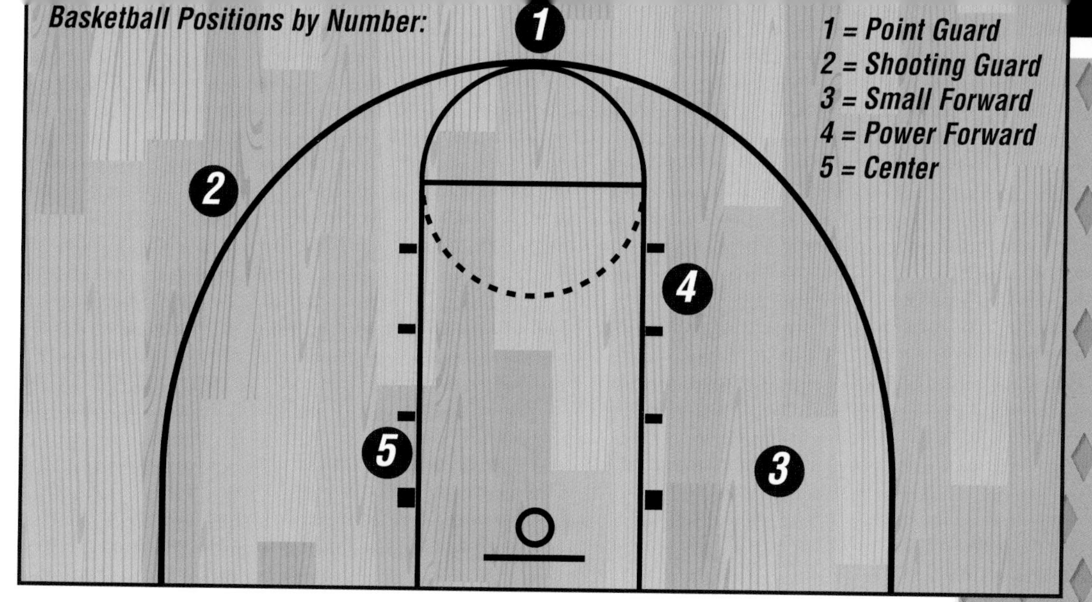

Coaches use these numbers to represent the five positions on the court.

*Basketball games start with a **jump ball** at mid court. The referee tosses the ball into the air and each team's center jumps to tap the ball toward a teammate.*

Centers usually position themselves on the edge of the **lane,** with their backs to the basket. If the center gets the ball, he uses a pivot move to face the basket and either shoot or pass.

Playmaker's FACT WITH IMPACT

The lanes on many basketball courts are painted. If someone says the center is playing in the paint, it doesn't mean he's using a brush. It just means he is in or near the lane, close to the basket.

GREATS of the GAME

Shaquille O'Neal is perhaps the most accomplished center currently playing pro basketball. He stands more than 7 feet (2.13 meters) tall and weighs nearly 350 pounds (159 kilograms). He has won four championships with two different teams. He was Rookie of the Year in 1993 and Most Valuable Player (MVP) in 2000. He is a 15-time NBA All-Star.

Skills with the Ball

Centers need to be sure-handed. When they receive a pass or grab a rebound, they need to **secure** the ball and either attempt to score, or pass to an open teammate. Centers perform **drills** to perfect their ability to catch the ball cleanly and protect it from their opponents.

Centers who can handle the ball in the open court are rare.

Some centers score by simply catching a rebound above their heads and immediately putting the ball back up toward the hoop. This is called a put-back since the player simply put a missed shot back in the basket.

Since they often do not face the basket, centers must be able to pivot with the ball. This involves spinning on one foot to face the **hoop** and then either shooting or passing. Pivoting is so important for centers; the position is sometimes called *playing the pivot.*

Playmaker's FACT WITH IMPACT

NBA Players with the All-Time Top Points Per Game Average

Name	Position	Points Per Game
Michael Jordan	*Guard*	*30.1*
Wilt Chamberlain	*Guard*	*30.1*
LeBron James	*Forward*	*27.5*
Elgin Baylor	*Forward*	*27.4*
Allen Iverson	*Guard*	*27.1*

Centers who can catch the ball, pivot, and shoot will have a chance to score many points.

No center had greater skills with the ball than Kareem Abdul Jabbar.

GREATS of the GAME

Kareem Abdul Jabbar began his pro career as Lew Alcindor. He changed his name while playing for the Milwaukee Bucks. He helped the Bucks win their only world championship in 1971. From 1975 until 1989 he played for the Los Angeles Lakers, where he won five more NBA titles. His sky-hook shot was nearly unstoppable. He scored more points than any other player in NBA history.

Skills on Defense

When on defense, centers usually stay near the basket and use their height to try blocking opponents' shots.

They need to be able to move short distances quickly in order to help defend against opponents who drive toward the basket and shoot.

Playmaker's FACT WITH IMPACT

Shots can only be blocked while they move upward toward the basket. Blocking a shot on its downward arc, or touching the basket, is a ***goaltending*** *violation. Goaltending mostly happens at the college or pro level where players are able to jump higher than the rim, which is 10 feet (3.05 meters) off the ground.*

***Shot blocking is a skill requiring height, timing, and body control. If the shot blocker makes contact with the shooter, the referee calls a* foul.**

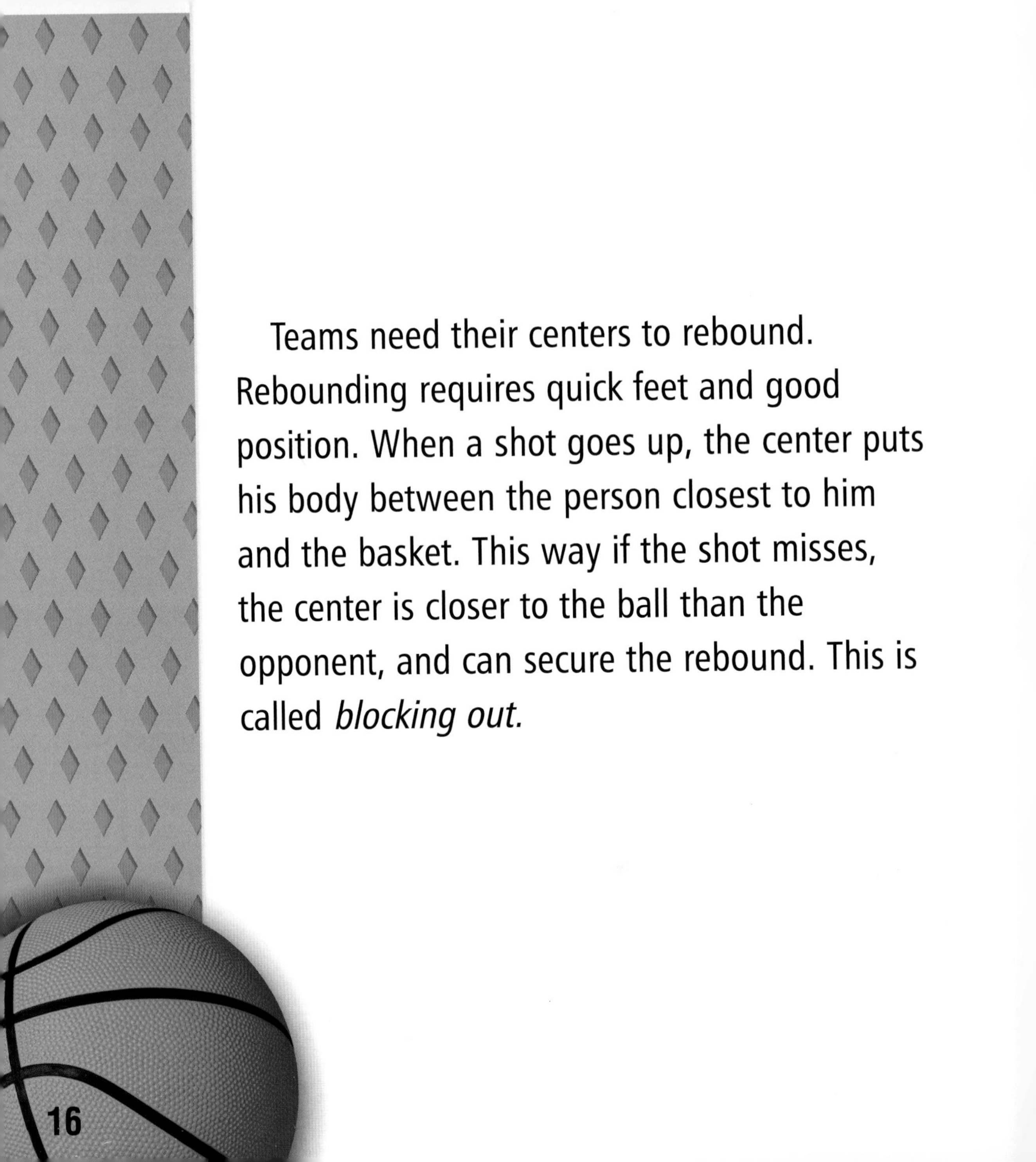

Teams need their centers to rebound. Rebounding requires quick feet and good position. When a shot goes up, the center puts his body between the person closest to him and the basket. This way if the shot misses, the center is closer to the ball than the opponent, and can secure the rebound. This is called *blocking out.*

A center will defend shots by putting a hand up, but will then turn his back to the shooter to block him from getting the rebound.

Wilt Chamberlain's defensive skills were so dominant, some of the rules of basketball were changed to make the game more fair.

GREATS of the GAME

Wilt Chamberlain's nickname was The Big Dipper *since, at more than 7 feet (2.13 meters) tall, he dipped his head to fit through doorways. He scored and rebounded like a machine. Because of his shot-blocking skills, goaltending became illegal. To keep him from getting almost every rebound, the league made the lane wider. During the 1962 season, he averaged 50 points and 25 rebounds a game and once actually scored 100 points in a game. Many basketball fans feel some of Wilt's records might never be broken.*

So You Want to Be a Center?

Prepare for action! Playing center means you'll need to score, rebound, and make it difficult for the opponent to score near the basket. You will need to practice catching the ball, pivoting, shooting, and passing.

Playmaker's FACT WITH IMPACT

Five fouls and you're out! Players get disqualified from games after committing a fifth foul. That means all players, but especially centers, need to learn how to play defense without fouling.

Most centers rarely dribble, and do most of their scoring right around the basket.

scorers and defenders near the basket.

If you are tall, willing to use your body to block out, and can catch the ball, pivot, and score, then you might one day find yourself patrolling the paint, manning the middle, or playing the pivot. In any case, you will stand out as your team's center!

Glossary

drills (DRILZ): repetitive exercises that teach specific skills

drive (DRIVE): when a player with the ball dribbles toward the basket

foul (FOUL): to bump, touch, hit, or make illegal contact with an opponent

goaltending (GOHL-ten-ding): touching the ball as it descends toward, or is touching, the basket

hoop (HOOP): another term for basket; a circular rim with a net attached

jump ball (JUHMP BAWL): when two opponents leap to tip the ball to a teammate after the referee tosses it into the air

lane (LAYN): the area of a basketball court directly under the baskets, between the free throw lines and the end lines

NBA (EN-BEE-AY): abbreviation for National Basketball Association, the major league of professional basketball

patrolling (puh-TROHL-ing): the act of guarding or protecting a certain area or space

pivot (PIV-uht): to swing around while keeping one foot on the floor, or the area of a basketball court near the basket where the center positions himself on offense

rebound (REE-bound): to grab the ball after a missed shot

secure (si-KYOOR): to bring something under one's control

Websites to Visit

www.nba.com
www.hoophall.com
www.basketball-reference.com

About the Author

Tom Greve lives in Chicago with his wife, Meg, and their two children, Madison and William. He enjoys playing, watching, and writing about sports.